Dave Ramsey's

Financial Peace® University

CHURCH COORDINATOR GUIDE

Mission Statement:

To empower and give HOPE to everyone from the financially secure to the financially distressed.

1749 Mallory Lane, Suite 100 • Brentwood, TN 37027.

Published by THE LAMPO GROUP, INC. For more information, please contact DAVE RAMSEY's office at 888.22.PEACE.

Dave Ramsey's
Financial Peace UNIVERSITY

Dear FPU Coordinator,

CONGRATULATIONS on becoming part of our team! We're thrilled that you've chosen to join us in fulfilling our mission to **"empower and give hope to everyone from the financially secure to the financially distressed."**

What you're doing is extremely important. You'll not only lead your class through questions and discussions about their personal finances, but more importantly, you'll listen to their stories, sympathize with their struggles, challenge them to break bad habits, and inspire them to change their family tree.

We know that talking about personal finances with a group of people can be intimidating, but just relax and be yourself. You won't have all the answers, but don't sweat it. If you open up and be honest and vulnerable about your specific situation, your class will do the same. Keep challenging them and you'll see powerful changes! Assure everyone that no matter what, you're there to listen, support, and guide.

After watching literally hundreds of thousands of families work through *Financial Peace University*, we've found that the average family **eliminates $5,300 in debt and saves $2,700 during the 13-week period**. That's a major turnaround! However, I'm not only talking about a financial turnaround. Throughout the process, lives are being changed, families are learning how to communicate about money, parents are learning how to teach their kids, and singles are developing the self-accountability needed for a successful life.

Get excited! You will watch as lives are transformed in your class, so be prepared to see chains broken, relationships restored, and hope revived.

Again, congratulations and welcome aboard Dave Ramsey's TEAM!

Louis Falzetti

Louis Falzetti, Executive Vice President
Financial Peace University
Colossians 3:23

Touching Lives...Changing a Nation!

877.378.2667 • daveramsey.com/church

TABLE OF CONTENTS

TOUCHING LIVES...CHANGING A NATION!

Personal finance is 80% behavior and only 20% head knowledge. Therefore, the goal of *Financial Peace University* isn't just information—it's transformation! We have found that absolutely nothing is more effective at changing behaviors than the properly-led small group. That's where you come in!

As you lead *Financial Peace University,* remember to:

Inspire Change!

As you lead your FPU class, you won't just watch other people change their lives—yours will change, too! As you grow more confident and competent in handling your money, pass on that excitement to your class members. You should all experience a dramatic personal transformation together!

Offer Hope!

Your enthusiasm and passion will be a major source of encouragement to the men and women in your class. Don't be afraid to show them your heart!

Get Intense!

Get wired up! Get fired up! Point out how debt has stolen your peace and caused you pain. Your example will increase everyone's intensity about freedom from debt.

Keep Up With Your Class!

Fill out your class roster every week. If anyone misses more than two classes, give him or her a call to check in and see if you can do anything to help.

Chop Your Plastic!

If you have any credit cards, you should be the first one to cut them up by the end of the fourth lesson. The group will feed off of your passion and commitment.

Join the Crusade!

FPU is not just another financial class—it's a movement to change this nation!

PREPARING FOR EACH CLASS SESSION

Review the Class Outline

Pay special attention to the "Remember to Bring" items and the "Small Group Discussion and Accountability" questions. These questions will make up the heart of your discussion time.

Preview the DVD

Make sure that the DVD lesson for that week plays with no problems whatsoever. If you do experience an issue with a lesson DVD, please contact your FPU Advisor immediately. If the DVD needs to be replaced, simply show another FPU lesson out of order until you receive a replacement.

Focus Your Thoughts Beforehand

We recommend praying for wisdom and understanding as you lead your FPU class. Also, pray that your class members will be receptive, empowered, and encouraged by the lesson and accountability discussion.

Gather Volunteers

Throughout the class, it will be helpful to have a ready source of volunteers to help facilitate the discussion. This is especially important if you have a large class. We recommend that large classes watch the video lesson together but then break up into separate discussion groups of 10-25 people. If you have such a class, you'll need volunteer facilitators to lead each of these smaller groups.

Prepare the Room

Arrange the chairs for watching the DVD and make sure your audio/visual equipment is in good working order. Also, have a supply of spare pens or pencils available in case someone needs one.

Be Gracious Guests

Before leaving after class, make sure the room is in excellent condition each week.

SMALL GROUP TECHNIQUES

Respect Everyone's Time

Because FPU inspires such great, enlightening, and often emotional conversations, it is easy to go past your allotted time frame. Be careful here! You have made a commitment to your class members that each week's class will be exactly two hours long. Always be aware of the time!

Reinforce the Need to Complete the Program

FPU is a full 13-week program. We know that 13 weeks can seem like a really long time! However, that amount of time is necessary to bring about the behavior change and the new habits that are vital to everyone's long-term success!

Therefore, from the very first lesson, be sure to emphasize how important it is that each class member attend every class and stick with the program all the way to the end!

Engage Interaction

Your job as a coordinator is to get everyone else to talk by facilitating the conversation. The members should hold one another accountable. If you're doing more than **10% of the talking, you're talking too much!**

Also, watch out for those who dominate the conversation and those who may seem hesitant to speak up at all. You'll need to make sure everyone has a chance to speak and that they feel free and comfortable doing so.

Encourage Openness

For genuine behavior change to take place, each member of your class must be willing to open up and truly be transparent in the discussion and accountability time. Everyone around the circle will take their cue from you. If you open up, listen intently to others, and use humor and personal stories, then they probably will, too.

Don't Fear Silence

Sometimes, you will have to sit in a moment of silence after asking a question. That's okay. Silence can be a powerful motivator. Try to fight the temptation to fill that void yourself, particularly after asking a difficult discussion question.

Show Compassion

Get excited about victories! Gently confront a member's unwillingness to change. And, don't be afraid to let someone cry if they're hurting. This is all part of the healing process. Show the class that you genuinely care about them.

Be Tactful

This class is "seeker friendly," so there is no need to "Bible thump." In fact, don't do it. Let them experience the Word of God through the lessons, realizing that God cares about their day-to-day lives in a personal, practical way. Then, in your small group, just be real and loving; let them see Jesus in your actions. If you are using FPU as a Bible study, feel free to incorporate more Scripture. However, if you are using FPU as an outreach, be sensitive, since some of these people are unchurched or may not have had a good experience with churches in the past.

Pray for the Class Members

Set aside a time once a week to pray for the members in your class. Most of them will be making big changes to their thinking and habits. God will empower their progress to financial peace! Pray for those who may not know Christ. Pray over the duration of the class for doors to be opened so they may discover a relationship with Jesus.

WRAPPING UP YOUR FPU CLASS

Coordinator Report

We want to know how your class went! Please let us know your successes, trials, and comments by completing the Coordinator Report online at the Coordinator Resource Center (daveramsey.com/fpucoordinator). If you cannot access the online form, you may also use the paper form at the back of this Coordinator Guide. Simply fax it to our office at 615.620.6398 after your last class session. We use the actual numbers and statistics from each class to learn how to better serve families like yours.

Start Another Class

Consider starting a new FPU class after your first 13-week class is finished. Leading multiple FPU classes will increase your intensity and impact more lives with the message of peace.

Help Others Start New FPU Classes

People who go through an FPU class often want to become class facilitators and start new classes. That's great! At the conclusion of your class, ask if anyone is interested in starting a new FPU class in their area.

Send Us Your Suggestions

If you have any ideas about how we can improve *Financial Peace University*, or if you have suggestions for future discussion questions or additional online resources, please let us know! Email us at fpu@daveramsey.com.

FREE ONLINE RESOURCES TO ASSIST YOU WITH YOUR FPU CLASS

Coordinator Resource Center (CRC) – daveramsey.com/fpucoordinator
At the CRC, you get the benefit of an online community for all your needs as an FPU Coordinator. You'll find:

- Useful forum discussions
- Free promo items
- Inspirational stories
- Access to important forms and guides
- Easy kit ordering options
- Creative class ideas

Member Resource Center (MRC) – daveramsey.com/fpumember
You and your class will love the many benefits of using the MRC! As an FPU member, you have FREE access throughout your 13-week class! You'll enjoy:

- Powerful budget software
- Active online discussion community
- Bonus articles, videos, and mini-lessons
- Customized supplements for every FPU lesson
- Up-to-date information, special offers, and prize drawings

My Total Money Makeover (MyTMMO) – daveramsey.com
MyTMMO provides even more tools, content, and an online community to keep you well-informed and equipped to answer your class' tough questions. As an FPU Coordinator, you can get your FREE one-year MyTMMO membership from your FPU Advisor or by reading the MyTMMO sign-up instructions at the Coordinator Resource Center.

Additional Online Resources

The MRC offers informative content, inspiring stories, helpful budgeting tools, and useful calculators. Members can even complete each week's homework at the MRC!

Follow these steps to introduce your class to the Member Resource Center:

1. Register your class online in the Coordinator Resource Center. An email with your class code will be sent to you once your class is confirmed.
2. If you cannot register your class online at this time, contact your FPU Advisor at 877.378.2667 to get your class code.
3. Write your class code in the space provided below.
4. During your first class session, have each member write the code in the space provided on page 13 of their member workbook. Your class can begin using this great FREE resource immediately.

YOUR FPU CLASS CODE:

If you are leading a class, you can get your class code by registering your class online or by contacting your FPU Advisor. Distribute this class code to your class members. If you are taking FPU as part of an individual home study, visit the Member Resource Center for details on how to register for your free membership.

To start using this FREE resource today, visit:

daveramsey.com/fpumember

This resource is provided to FPU members by Dave Ramsey's My Total Money Makeover.

How to Use the Weekly Class Guides

The weekly class guides on the following pages will walk you week by week through the FPU program. We recommend that you have your own member workbook and the weekly class guide open and easily accessible during each class discussion.

In these guides, you will find:

- A class schedule, showing approximately how much time to devote to each portion of the night's activities.
- Weekly review questions to reinforce what was discussed the previous week.*
- Small group discussion and accountability questions that guide your class members through an in-depth discussion of each week's key concepts and ensure that they are making the necessary behavior changes throughout the program.*
- Weekly budget checks, which call for every class member to hold their budgets in the air and reaffirm their commitment to stick to their plan.
- Time to share weekly victory stories, which gives your class members a chance to update the group on any special milestones or accomplishments from the previous week.
- A five-minute wrap-up with homework reminders, reading assignments, and a review of all the lesson-specific bonus material that is available online in the Member Resource Center for that week.*

It's that easy! We've given you everything you need to successfully guide your class step by step through FPU. Now, all you need to do is add a dose of intensity, a sense of humor, and a little compassion—and prepare to team up with a group of people who are ready to get weird and change their lives!

*Note: The weekly review, discussion and accountability questions, and homework reminders are exactly what appear on that week's "Discussion and Accountability" page in the member workbook. That way, you can see exactly what they see in their workbooks.

Dave Ramsey's

Financial Peace®

UNIVERSITY

Weekly Class Guides

Remember to Bring:

- Membership kits for each family
- Attendance Roster (from back of this guide)
- Pens or pencils
- FPU DVD disc 1, *Super Saving*

After watching the video lesson, be sure to rearrange the chairs into a circle for the discussion and accountability time. This creates more intimate discussions, as each member can see everyone else's face and maintain eye contact with the person speaking.

5 minutes Welcome To FPU!

Greet every class member as they walk in for the first time. As you hand out their membership kits, take a moment to introduce yourself and briefly explain how the class time will be spent each week.

You should always reinforce the need to complete the course. On average, about 80% of your class will graduate. You can improve this percentage by encouraging everyone early and often to complete the class. Also, it is never too early to start planting seeds for your class members to start a new class in the future!

60 minutes Watch *Super Saving* DVD

Have class members turn to page 15 of the member workbook.

10 minutes Introductions

Have your class members introduce themselves by answering the introduction questions on page 27 of the member workbook. Take the lead by introducing yourself first. If you have a personal FPU success story to share, go ahead and let everyone know!

40 minutes Small Group Discussion and Accountability

Respond to the following discussion questions (from page 27 of the member workbook), sharing openly and giving personal illustrations when possible. Be honest and real with each other.

1. What is keeping you from saving?
2. What is Baby Step 1? Why is this important?
3. Why do so many people use debt (credit cards, loans, etc.) for emergencies? Have you ever done this? Be honest!

4. Read Genesis 41:35-36. What does this tell us about the importance of saving money?

5. According to Proverbs 21:20, what does a foolish man do? In what ways do we often do the same thing as this foolish man?

6. Dave talked about how money is amoral using the analogy of the brick. What did this illustration mean to you? Have you ever thought of money as being "good" or "bad" in and of itself?

7. What does "Murphy Repellant" mean? If you had some savings built up, do you think you'd have fewer emergencies?

8. Statistics show that most of us will have a major, unexpected, negative financial event in any 10-year period. What would constitute a "negative financial event" in your situation? How would you handle that today?

9. How would it feel if you had savings to cover an emergency? How would that change your attitude when unexpected things happen?

5 minutes Wrap Up

Homework Reminder (from page 27 of the member workbook)

1. Complete the Basic Quickie Budget form and bring this to class next week.
2. Register for the Member Resource Center (MRC).
3. Read *Financial Peace Revisited,* chapters 1, 2, 3, and 10.

Online Features

Remind everyone to take advantage of the special online resources for *Super Saving* at daveramsey.com/fpumember.

online resources™

Be sure to check out the special online features for this week.

- **Financial Reality Check:** Find out where your current financial plan will lead you!
- **Emergency Fund Tracker:** How fast can you save your first $1,000?
- **Drive Free, Retire Rich:** Discover the best way to buy a car!
- **Private Journal:** Record your progress in your own private journal!

Class members to check up on this week:

Remember to Bring:

- Attendance Roster
- Pens or pencils
- FPU DVD disc 2, *Relating With Money*

5 minutes Review of Last Week

Review questions taken from page 35 of the member workbook:

1. Name three reasons why you should save money.
2. What is Baby Step 1? Why is it important to do this first?
3. What can you do to fund your emergency fund quickly?
4. Everyone hold up your completed Basic Quickie Budget form. We told you we'd check to see if you did it!

60 minutes Watch *Relating With Money* DVD

Have class members turn to page 29 of the member workbook.

3 minutes Class Commitments

Review the class commitments presented on page 35 of the member workbook:

1. Make a verbal commitment to start putting something aside for an emergency fund every month, even if it is only $4.
2. Commit to attend all 13 class sessions.

When checking everyone's Basic Quickie Budget form this week, play it up with some excitement! Have some fun with it, but make it clear that the class is expected to bring their budgets with them every week from now on.

45 minutes Small Group Discussion and Accountability

Form a circle and discuss these questions from page 35 of the member workbook:

1. How can working together on a budget help your family follow God's leading and effectively plan for the future?
2. What are the advantages to being single in regards to financial control? What are the disadvantages?
3. What are some of the reasons that finances should be agreed upon by both partners in a marriage?

4. Do you put relationships above money, making your spouse, children, and friends more important than financial stress? Would others agree with your answer?
5. What are some practical ways to teach your kids about money?
6. Proverbs 22:6 says, "Train up a child in the way he should go." Then, verse 7 says, "The rich rule over the poor and the borrower is servant to the lender." How are these two verses related?
7. Respond to this statement: "How you spend your money tells me who you are and what is important to you."
8. How do fatigue and stress affect your money management?
9. Say aloud: "I did not get into financial stress quickly, and I will most likely walk out of it slowly."

5 minutes Weekly Victory Story

Ask: Who has a special victory story to share this week?

Example: completed a Baby Step, paid off a debt, got a great bargain, had an emotional or relational breakthrough with money, etc.

2 minutes Wrap Up

Homework Reminder (from page 35 of the member workbook)

1. Goal for the week: identify a reliable accountability partner.
2. Start collecting credit card offers that come in the mail.
3. Read *Financial Peace Revisited,* chapters 14-18.

Online Features

Remind everyone to take advantage of the special online resources for *Relating With Money* at daveramsey.com/fpumember.

online resources™

Be sure to check out the special online features for this week.

- **Learn the Rules:** Download and print a copy of Dave's rules for the "Budget Committee Meeting."
- **Video:** Rachel Ramsey reveals "Five Reasons Why It's So Tough Being Dave Ramsey's Kid"!
- **Junior's Clubhouse:** Dave has a website just for kids! Games, stories, and other resources entertain while teaching important lessons about money.

Class members to check up on this week:

____

____

____

____

____

____

____

____

Remember to Bring:

- 3 x 5 index cards
- Attendance Roster
- Pens or pencils
- FPU DVD disc 3, *Cash Flow Planning*

5 minutes Review of Last Week

Review questions taken from page 61 of the member workbook:

1. The flow of money represents your family's:
   A. Income B. Value System C. Teamwork
2. Explain the concept of the Nerd and Free Spirit.
3. Who should do the financial decision-making in a marriage?
4. How can an accountability partner help a single person win with money?

64 minutes Watch *Cash Flow Planning* DVD

Have class members turn to page 37 of the member workbook.

Encourage married couples to work together on their budgets.

Remind them of the "Budget Committee Meeting" rules we learned last week. Singles should discuss their first budget with the accountability partner they've already selected.

40 minutes Small Group Discussion and Accountability

Form a circle and discuss these questions from page 61 of the member workbook:

1. Read Proverbs 3:20-22. When planning out the budget for the month, how can you use "sound wisdom and discretion"?
2. What are the benefits of a written cash flow plan? Be specific. How can this impact a marriage? How can it strengthen a single person?
3. What things have kept you from living on a cash flow plan?
4. Read Matthew 6:21. How does the budgeting process show where our hearts are?
5. What are some reasons why you've always hated the idea of a budget? What are your initial reactions to the concept?
6. How can the concept of the Four Walls (food, shelter, clothing, transportation) empower you to prioritize your spending?

7. When have you been guilty of letting someone else set your family's financial priorities? Explain.
8. How well do you understand the cash envelope system? In what areas of your budget could you implement this immediately?
9. Why is it important to set aside a little "blow money" every month?

3 minutes Class Debt Exercise

Pass out 3 x 5 index cards. Have each family anonymously write down their total debt (not including a mortgage). Collect the cards and add up the total debt load of the class. Share this with everyone and let them know that you'll do this again at the end of FPU so you can all see how far you've come!

3 minutes Weekly Victory Story

Ask: Who has a special victory story to share this week?

Example: completed a Baby Step, paid off a debt, got a great bargain, had an emotional or relational breakthrough with money, etc.

5 minutes Wrap Up

Homework Reminder (from page 61 of the member workbook)

1. Review your credit report.
2. Read *Financial Peace Revisited,* chapters 19 and 21.

Online Features

Remind everyone to take advantage of the special online resources for *Cash Flow Planning* at daveramsey.com/fpumember.

online resources™

Be sure to check out the special online features for this week.

- **Financial Snapshot:** Track your progress with this quick online form.
- **Gazelle Budget Software:** Create and maintain your budget with our exclusive online software!
- **Budget Forms:** Download printable copies of all the forms discussed in this lesson.
- **Checkbook Help:** Get a quick refresher on how to balance your checking account!
- **Free Podcast:** Get a daily dose of Dave!

Class members to check up on this week:

____

____

____

____

____

____

Remember to Bring:

- Scissors for cutting up credit cards
- Credit cards if you have any to cut up
- Glass jar for credit card pieces
- Attendance Roster
- Pens or pencils
- FPU DVD disc 4, *Dumping Debt*

This video is longer than the other lessons. Be sure to start on time so that you'll have enough time at the end of the video to review the discussion questions and cut up some credit cards!

5 minutes Review of Last Week

Review questions taken from page 75 of the member workbook:

1. What is a zero-based budget? Why is it important?
2. Name one of the three reasons we need to do a zero-based budget each month.
3. Hold your budget up! How did your first family budget session go?

100 minutes Watch *Dumping Debt* DVD

Have class members turn to page 63 of the member workbook.

10 minutes Small Group Discussion and Accountability

Form a circle and discuss these questions from page 75 of the member workbook:

1. How old were you when you got your first credit card? How did that make you feel (at the time)?
2. Does debt limit your ability to serve God? If so, how?
3. What would it feel like to have absolutely no debt?
4. Discuss Proverbs 6:1-5 and the formula for getting out of debt. How can you begin applying this truth in your life?
5. Think about all the money that is currently going out in the form of debt payments (credit cards, furniture, car loan, mortgage, etc.). What could you do with all that money every month if you actually got to keep it?
6. Do you currently have or have you ever had a debt CONsolidation loan? Did you discover that it really was a con?
7. Have you ever believed or spread any of the myths covered in this lesson? Which ones?

8. Why is "gazelle intensity" so important in getting out of debt?
9. What is your reaction to the phrase "the borrower is slave to the lender"?
10. Do you have any questions about the debt snowball?

3 minutes Cut Up Credit Cards!

Chop some plastic this week! Ask if anyone wants to cut up their credit cards in front of the class. If you have any yourself, you should be the first to cut them up! Put the pieces in a glass jar and try to fill it up throughout the remaining weeks of the class. Make this a regular opportunity every week from now on.

2 minutes Wrap Up

Homework Reminder (from page 75 of the member workbook)

1. Complete the Credit Card History form.
2. Complete the Debt Snowball form.
3. Read *Financial Peace Revisited*, chapters 7 and 8.

Online Features

Remind everyone to take advantage of the special online resources for *Dumping Debt* at daveramsey.com/fpumember.

online resources™

Be sure to check out the special online features for this week.

- **Debt Snowball Software:** Track your progress and calculate your DEBT FREE date!
- **Drive Free, Retire Rich:** Discover the best way to buy a car.

Class members to check up on this week:

____

____

____

____

____

____

____

____

Remember to Bring:

- Scissors for cutting up credit cards
- Glass jar for credit card pieces
- Attendance Roster
- Pens or pencils
- FPU DVD disc 5, *Credit Sharks In Suits*

5 minutes Review of Last Week

Review questions taken from page 97 of the member workbook:

1. What are the six steps to getting out of debt?
2. What are the seven Baby Steps (in order)?
3. Why is it important to complete Baby Step 1 before moving on to Baby Step 2?

62 minutes Watch *Credit Sharks In Suits* DVD

Have class members turn to page 77 of the member workbook.

45 minutes Small Group Discussion and Accountability

Form a circle and discuss these questions from page 97 of the member workbook:

1. For those of you who have been contacted by a collector or creditor, what emotions have you experienced?
2. Look at Proverbs 22:1. How do many collection agencies make us feel about our "good name"?
3. In what way is *emotion* a collector's best weapon?
4. Have you ever let a collector set your family's priorities?
5. What are the "Four Walls"? Why is it important to always pay necessities first before paying your creditors, such as credit card companies?
6. True or False: A collector can garnish your wages at any time.
7. Has anyone here been a victim of identity theft? How has that impacted your life?

As we talk about collection practices in this lesson, you may discover that someone in your class is facing unbelievable pressure from a bill collector. Make a note of any class member that needs extra encouragement and be sure to follow up this week.

2 minutes Weekly Budget Check

Have every class member hold up their budget. Does anyone have any questions they need to ask about their budget?

3 minutes Weekly Victory Story

Ask: Who has a special victory story to share this week?

Example: completed a Baby Step, paid off a debt, got a great bargain, had an emotional or relational breakthrough with money, etc.

3 minutes Wrap Up

Homework Reminder (from page 97 of the member workbook)

1. Review your credit report.
2. Read *Financial Peace Revisited,* chapters 9 and 22.

Online Features

Remind everyone to take advantage of the special online resources for *Credit Sharks In Suits* at daveramsey.com/fpumember.

online resources™

Be sure to check out the special online features for this week.

- **Free Credit Report:** Learn how to get a free copy of your credit report online every year.
- **National Do Not Call List:** Stop those annoying telemarketer calls with the U.S. National Do Not Call Registry.
- **Prescreen Opt-Out:** End all of the "pre-approved" credit offers that fill up your mailbox by automatically turning away any company that tries to check your credit without your knowledge.
- **Identity Theft Protection:** Find out about the only ID theft protection that Dave recommends.

Class members to check up on this week:

____

____

____

____

____

Remember to Bring:

- Scissors for cutting up credit cards
- Glass jar for credit card pieces
- Attendance Roster
- Pens or pencils
- FPU DVD disc 6, *Buyer Beware*

5 minutes Review of Last Week

Review questions taken from page 103 of the member workbook:

1. What are collectors trained to do?
2. Who should set the priorities for your family—you or the collectors?
3. How often should you check your credit report? Why?
4. What are the Four Walls?
5. Name the seven Baby Steps in order.

56 minutes Watch *Buyer Beware* DVD

Have class members turn to page 99 of the member workbook.

50 minutes Small Group Discussion and Accountability

Form a circle and discuss these questions from page 103 of the member workbook:

1. Proverbs 1:5 says, "A man of understanding will acquire wise counsel." What are some ways we can "acquire wise counsel" before a major purchase?
2. How do marketers use emotion to compel you to purchase their goods?
3. How can waiting overnight before making a purchase change your behavior? Would you have as much debt now if you had always waited overnight?
4. How would you define a "major purchase"? Why is it so important for married couples to agree on major purchases?
5. What can singles do to guard themselves against impulsive buying decisions?

This lesson underscores the importance of couples working together and singles working with an accountability partner. Make sure your class members have someone with whom to discuss their finances.

6. How can you ensure that you will genuinely enjoy your purchases?
7. True or False: I do not borrow money anymore, including using credit cards. Why or why not?
8. In what ways has having an accountability partner been helpful to you? Do you still need help in this area?

1 minute Weekly Budget Check

Have every class member hold up their budget. Does anyone have any questions they need to ask about their budget?

3 minutes Weekly Victory Story

Ask: Who has a special victory story to share this week?

Example: completed a Baby Step, paid off a debt, got a great bargain, had an emotional or relational breakthrough with money, etc.

5 minutes Wrap Up

Homework Reminder (from page 103 of the member workbook)

1. Complete your second Financial Snapshot.
2. Memorize the five keys to gaining power over your purchases.
3. Read *Financial Peace Revisited,* chapter 5.

Online Features

Remind everyone to take advantage of the special online resources for *Buyer Beware* at daveramsey.com/fpumember.

daveramsey.com/fpumember

online resources™

Be sure to check out the special online features for this week.

- **Stupid Tax Forum:** Laugh with others as you share your own stupid tax stories!
- **Do Not Call List:** End the dinner time telemarketing calls by adding yourself to the national "Do Not Call" list.
- **Buyer Beware Testimonies:** Listen to some great Buyer Beware stories we've collected from other FPU members.

Class members to check up on this week:

____

____

____

____

____

____

____

____

Remember to Bring:

- Scissors for cutting up credit cards
- Glass jar for credit card pieces
- Attendance Roster
- Pens or pencils
- FPU DVD disc 7, *Clause and Effect*

We're now seven weeks into our 13-week program. Keep your class' commitment level high by stressing the importance of completing all 13 weeks of FPU. We still have a lot of ground to cover!

4 minutes Review of Last Week

Review questions taken from page 113 of the member workbook:

1. Name five keys to power over purchase. Did you discuss these things with your spouse or accountability partner this week?
2. Complete this statement: "FPU has helped my life by...."

64 minutes Watch *Clause and Effect* DVD

Have class members turn to page 105 of the member workbook.

45 minutes Small Group Discussion and Accountability

Form a circle and discuss these questions from page 113 of the member workbook:

1. What do you do if money is tight?
   A. Drop your insurance until you've paid off your debts.
   B. Put insurance only on the person who brings home the most income and pray nothing happens to the rest of the family.
   C. Make insurance a priority to avoid a financial disaster.
2. What could happen to you financially if you do not have the proper amount of insurance in place?
3. How does having an emergency fund affect your insurance premiums and deductibles?
4. What is the difference between term and cash value life insurance?
5. What happens to your cash savings inside of a cash value life insurance plan when you die?
6. Why is it so important to make sure your homeowner's policy includes guaranteed replacement cost?

7. Read 1 Timothy 5:8 together. How does insurance fit into this verse?

8. Why do you think so few people carry long-term disability coverage? Why is this so dangerous?

2 minutes Weekly Budget Check

Have every class member hold up their budget. Does anyone have any questions they need to ask about their budget?

3 minutes Weekly Victory Story

Ask: Who has a special victory story to share this week?

Example: completed a Baby Step, paid off a debt, got a great bargain, had an emotional or relational breakthrough with money, etc.

2 minutes Wrap Up

Homework Reminder (from page 113 of the member workbook)

1. Complete the Insurance Coverage Recap form.
2. Identify any insurance policies that need to be changed or added.
3. Calculate how much life insurance you need.
4. Read *Financial Peace Revisited,* chapter 11 (only the subtitled section "Insurance").

Online Features

Remind everyone to take advantage of the special online resources for *Clause and Effect* at daveramsey.com/fpumember.

online resources™

Be sure to check out the special online features for this week.

- **Identity Theft Protection:** Learn more about the ID theft policy that Dave recommends.
- **Get Help:** Find a reliable health insurance representative in your area with the heart of a teacher. If you need help, check out Dave's Endorsed Local Provider network.
- **Bonus Video:** Watch as Dave takes a call on the radio show from a listener with insurance questions.
- **Testimonies:** Read how others learned these insurance lessons—the hard way!

Class members to check up on this week:

____

____

____

____

____

____

____

Remember to Bring:

- Scissors for cutting up credit cards
- Glass jar for credit card pieces
- Attendance Roster
- Pens or pencils
- FPU DVD disc 8, *That's Not Good Enough!*

Since cash is a major discussion point for this lesson, this would be a great opportunity to see how everyone is doing with the cash envelope system. Bring your own envelopes to class and discuss how helpful this system has been for you.

5 minutes Review of Last Week

Review questions taken from page 121 of the member workbook:

1. The purpose of insurance is to:
   A. Lower risk B. Transfer risk C. Eliminate risk
2. True or False: Insurance is an essential planning tool. Why or why not?
3. At what point in the Baby Steps should insurance be included in your financial plan?
4. Hold up your monthly zero-based budget.
   A. Discuss how much easier or difficult it was to do this time compared to the first one. Be *honest* with each other.
   B. Discuss what you have learned about handling money.

59 minutes Watch *That's Not Good Enough!* DVD

Have class members turn to page 115 of the member workbook.

45 minutes Small Group Discussion and Accountability

Form a circle and discuss these questions from page 121 of the member workbook:

1. How can searching for big bargains help us be better managers of the resources God has given us?
2. Why do most people avoid negotiating for deals?
3. Describe a time when you found a great bargain. Was it a win-win?
4. Read Proverbs 17:20. What are some of the potential consequences of not being honest when bargaining? What good comes from telling the truth when you are bargaining? What are the seven rules of negotiating?

5. How could a business benefit from applying these techniques?
6. How often do you actually ask for a deal when shopping?
7. When you are at the store and the cashier gives you too much money back, what do you do?
   A. Keep it and don't say anything. B. Return it immediately.
8. Are you still plagued by impulse purchases? What goes through your heart and mind when you are tempted to spend?
9. How is your envelope system coming along? Are you sticking to your written budget?

2 minutes Weekly Budget Check

Have every class member hold up their budget. Does anyone have any questions they need to ask about their budget?

4 minutes Weekly Victory Story

Ask: Who has a special victory story to share this week?

Example: completed a Baby Step, paid off a debt, got a great bargain, had an emotional or relational breakthrough with money, etc.

5 minutes Wrap Up

Homework Reminder (from page 121 of the member workbook)

1. Tell a friend about FPU.
2. Read *Financial Peace Revisited*, chapter 13.

Online Features

Remind everyone to take advantage of the special online resources for *That's Not Good Enough!* at daveramsey.com/fpumember.

online resources™

Be sure to check out the special online features for this week.

- **Bargain Bragging:** Hear other FPU students' bargain hunting success stories!
- **Online Deals:** Check out some great places for online deals and peer reviews.

Class members to check up on this week:

____

____

____

____

____

____

____

____

Remember to Bring:

- Scissors for cutting up credit cards
- Glass jar for credit card pieces
- Attendance Roster
- Pens or pencils
- FPU DVD disc 9, *Of Mice and Mutual Funds*

This lesson contains more technical details than most of the FPU videos. If you anticipate more questions from your class on this topic, you may want to review the entire lesson beforehand to make sure you understand the concepts presented.

5 minutes Review of Last Week

Review questions taken from page 131 of the member workbook:

1. What are the seven basic rules of negotiating?
2. Did the previous lesson change any of your shopping habits this week?

63 minutes Watch *Of Mice and Mutual Funds* DVD

Have class members turn to page 123 of the member workbook.

45 minutes Small Group Discussion and Accountability

Form a circle and discuss these questions from page 131 of the member workbook:

1. According to Proverbs 28:20, who abounds with blessings? What happens to "he who hastens to be rich"?
2. Explain what a mutual fund is and how it works.
3. Why is it dangerous to invest with borrowed money?
4. Read Ecclesiastes 11:2. According to this verse, how does diversification help us and why is it important?
5. Why are single stocks so dangerous?
6. Why does Dave stress the importance of becoming debt free (except the mortgage) before you begin your long-term investing?
7. Why is it so important to make your own educated, well-informed decisions, rather than simply surrendering your decisions to an advisor?
8. Talk about how important it is for spouses to be on the same page when it comes to dumping debt and investing.

2 minutes Weekly Budget Check

Have every class member hold up their budget. Does anyone have any questions they need to ask about their budget?

3 minutes Weekly Victory Story

Ask: Who has a special victory story to share this week?

Example: completed a Baby Step, paid off a debt, got a great bargain, had an emotional or relational breakthrough with money, etc.

2 minutes Wrap Up

Homework Reminder (from page 131 of the member workbook)

1. Calculate how much your debt payments are robbing from your retirement.
2. Complete your third Financial Snapshot.
3. Read *Financial Peace Revisited,* chapter 11 (only through the subtitled section "Simple Discipline Is the Key") and chapter 12 (only through the subtitled section "To Load or Not to Load").

Online Features

Remind everyone to take advantage of the special online resources for *Of Mice and Mutual Funds* at daveramsey.com/fpumember.

online resources™

Be sure to check out the special online features for this week.

- **Millionaire Calculator:** Discover what a one-time investment now could mean for your retirement!
- **Dave's Investment Strategy:** See exactly what Dave does—and does not do—with his own investment money.
- **Investment Calculator:** Learn the impact of inflation on your savings and investing with our online calculators and money tools!

Class members to check up on this week:

____

____

____

____

____

____

____

____

Remember to Bring:

- Scissors for cutting up credit cards
- Glass jar for credit card pieces
- Attendance Roster
- Pens or pencils
- FPU DVD disc 10, *From Fruition To Tuition*

This lesson covers two important Baby Steps. Be sure to continually review the Baby Steps with your class and stress the importance of doing them in order.

5 minutes Review of Last Week

Review questions taken from page 145 of the member workbook:

1. What does diversification mean and how does it affect your risk in investing?
2. Are mutual funds for long-term or short-term investing?
3. Explain Dave's four-fold diversification strategy for long-term investing.

57 minutes Watch *From Fruition To Tuition* DVD

Have class members turn to page 133 of the member workbook.

48 minutes Small Group Discussion and Accountability

Form a circle and discuss these questions from page 145 of the member workbook:

1. Ask someone to read Proverbs 13:22. What is one thing the Bible asks us to do for future generations?
2. What do you think when you see retirement-aged people working in grocery stores? Is that what you want to do when you retire?
3. What motivates you to get serious about your retirement plan?
4. Should you ever temporarily stop adding to your retirement plan? If so, why? When should you start up again?
5. Does college funding come before or after retirement savings according to the Baby Steps? Why?

6. Would you feel guilty taking care of your own retirement plan before putting money aside for your child's college education?
7. How can retirement planning free you to serve the Kingdom of God in your golden years?
8. How does living by a monthly budget help you prepare for retirement?

2 minutes Weekly Budget Check

Have every class member hold up their budget. Does anyone have any questions they need to ask about their budget?

3 minutes Weekly Victory Story

Ask: Who has a special victory story to share this week?

Example: completed a Baby Step, paid off a debt, got a great bargain, had an emotional or relational breakthrough with money, etc.

5 minutes Wrap Up

Homework Reminder (from page 145 of the member workbook)

1. Complete the Monthly Retirement Planning form.
2. Complete the Monthly College Planning form.
3. Read *Financial Peace Revisited,* chapter 12 (beginning with the subtitled section "Funding Those Golden Rocking Chairs").

Online Features

Remind everyone to take advantage of the special online resources for *From Fruition To Tuition* at daveramsey.com/fpumember.

online resources™

Be sure to check out the special online features for this week.

- **Investment Calculator:** Find out how much you need to save to retire with dignity and independence.
- **Get Investment Help:** Find an investment professional in your area with the heart of a teacher. If you need help, check out our network of Endorsed Local Providers.
- **Extra Forms:** Download printable worksheets to calculate the monthly savings needed for your retirement and college planning goals.

Class members to check up on this week:

____

____

____

____

____

____

____

____

Remember to Bring:
- Scissors for cutting up credit cards
- Glass jar for credit card pieces
- Attendance Roster
- Pens or pencils
- FPU DVD disc 11, *Working In Your Strengths*

As we discuss careers, be sure not to overlook stay-at-home moms. These hard workers perform the most challenging and rewarding job of all!

5 minutes Review of Last Week

Review questions taken from page 155 of the member workbook:

1. What is an IRA?
2. Should you ever cash in or borrow against pre-taxed retirement savings early to pay off debt? Why or why not?

50 minutes Watch *Working In Your Strengths* DVD

Have class members turn to page 147 of the member workbook.

55 minutes Small Group Discussion and Accountability

Form a circle and discuss these questions from page 155 of the member workbook:

1. If you could do anything you wanted and money was no object, what would you do? How is your current work preparing you to do that?
2. God has a plan and future for your life. Why, then, do many people stay in a job they do not feel called to or even enjoy?
3. What areas of growth or education will help you along your career path?
4. Based on your unique personality, what strengths do you bring to the workplace?
5. Answer to yourself—True or False: I am supportive of my spouse's work and encourage him/her for all the hard work he/she does to help provide for the family.
6. Talk about the danger of being a workaholic. How can it affect your life, spirit, and family? Is this a non-issue if you are single?
7. Have you tried any creative home-based business ideas?

8. Discuss some benefits of temporarily working a second job to pay off debts with gazelle intensity.
9. Read Proverbs 23:4-5 together. According to the verse, why should we not set our eyes on riches?
10. Have you stopped using credit cards for purchases?

2 minutes Weekly Budget Check

Have every class member hold up their budget. Does anyone have any questions they need to ask about their budget?

3 minutes Weekly Victory Story

Ask: Who has a special victory story to share this week?

Example: completed a Baby Step, paid off a debt, got a great bargain, had an emotional or relational breakthrough with money, etc.

5 minutes Wrap Up

Homework Reminder (from page 155 of the member workbook)

1. Review the DISC chart in the member workbook to determine if your current line of work naturally fits within your unique personality style.
2. Lay out a three-year professional plan.
3. Read *Financial Peace Revisited,* chapter 6.

Online Features

Remind everyone to take advantage of the special online resources for *Working In Your Strengths* at daveramsey.com/fpumember.

online resources™

Be sure to check out the special online features for this week.

- **Radio Excerpt:** Listen in as Dave talks to a radio listener about whether or not he should leave his job for another opportunity.
- **Free Podcast:** Don't forget to download one free hour of *The Dave Ramsey Show* every day!

Class members to check up on this week:

____

____

____

____

____

____

____

____

Remember to Bring:

- Scissors for cutting up credit cards
- Glass jar for credit card pieces
- Attendance Roster
- Pens or pencils
- FPU DVD disc 12, *Real Estate and Mortgages*

Next week is the final lesson! Give everyone on the class role a call this week to make sure that they'll be there to celebrate the completion of FPU!

5 minutes Review of Last Week

Review questions taken from page 169 of the member workbook:

1. What are some specific ways in which your unique personality style impacts your work life?
2. Discuss the three-year professional plan you outlined for yourself last week.
3. Why is sacrifice so important in taking on a part-time job for short-term goals?
4. Recite all seven Baby Steps.

63 minutes Watch *Real Estate and Mortgages* DVD

Have class members turn to page 157 of the member workbook.

45 minutes Small Group Discussion and Accountability

Form a circle and discuss these questions from page 169 of the member workbook:

1. Why is "counting the cost" before you build a house important?
2. Why should that "cost" also include having an emergency fund left over after the purchase of your home?
3. What does it mean to be "house poor"? Is anyone here in that situation?
4. Is it ever okay to rent for a while? Why or why not?
5. Have you ever been late on a mortgage payment? If so, how did that make you feel?
6. What are the dangers in 30-year mortgages, adjustable rate loans, and home equity loans?

7. If you have to take out a mortgage, what guidelines does Dave recommend? According to those principles, how much house can you actually afford?
8. How would paying off your home early make you feel? How would it affect your retirement?

2 minutes Weekly Budget Check

Have every class member hold up their budget. Does anyone have any questions they need to ask about their budget?

3 minutes Weekly Victory Story

Ask: Who has a special victory story to share this week?

Example: completed a Baby Step, paid off a debt, got a great bargain, had an emotional or relational breakthrough with money, etc.

2 minutes Wrap Up

Homework Reminder (from page 169 of the member workbook)

1. Complete your final Financial Snapshot.
2. Plan a graduation party for next week!
3. Read *Financial Peace Revisited*, chapter 13 (only the subtitled sections "Real Estate Bargains" and "Owner Financing Bonanza").

Online Features

Remind everyone to take advantage of the special online resources for *Real Estate and Mortgages* at daveramsey.com/fpumember.

online resources™

Be sure to check out the special online features for this week.

- **Easy Payoff Calculator:** See how quickly you can pay off your mortgage!
- **Mortgage Calculator:** Find out how much house you can actually afford.
- **Get Help:** Ready to buy or sell a home? Find a local realtor with the heart of a teacher. If you need help, you can contact one of Dave's Endorsed Local Providers in your area.
- **Check Your Math:** Learn why it's a bad idea to keep a mortgage just for a tax deduction.

Class members to check up on this week:

____

____

____

____

____

____

Remember to Bring:

- 3 x 5 index cards
- Scissors for cutting up credit cards
- Glass jar for credit card pieces
- Attendance Roster
- Pens or pencils
- Party supplies
- FPU DVD disc 13, *The Great Misunderstanding*

5 minutes Class Party

Have everyone fix a plate of food for the class party. Members should take their food to their seats for class.

5 minutes Review of Last Week

Review questions taken from page 177 of the member workbook:

1. Homes in good neighborhoods appreciate and are priced on what three standards?
2. True or False: The time and money you spend fixing up your house prior to selling can greatly increase your asking price.
3. According to Financial Peace principles, is it wiser to buy a little less house with a 15-year mortgage or more house with a 30-year mortgage?
4. Which is better, an adjustable or fixed-rate mortgage?

60 minutes Watch *The Great Misunderstanding* DVD

Have class members turn to page 171 of the member workbook.

40 minutes Small Group Discussion and Accountability

Form a circle and discuss these questions from page 177 of the member workbook:

1. Discuss the term "stewardship" in light of tonight's lesson.
2. Read Malachi 3:10-12 and discuss the word "blessing" with this lesson in mind. What do you think that word means?
3. Why don't we give as much as we'd like to at times?
4. How do you feel when you give?
5. Has anyone ever surprised you with a meaningful act of giving? How did that make you feel?
6. Why is it important to give while paying off debts?

Party time! Get to class a little early this week to set up a table for the food and party items that your class members will bring.

7. How does viewing yourself as a manager of God's resources affect your thinking and behavior about money?
8. What's the most important lesson you've learned in FPU?
9. In what ways has your life changed as a result of getting your money under control?
10. Have the spiritual principles of this program helped you seek God and His will for your life?

3 minutes Class Debt Exercise

Pass out 3 x 5 index cards. Have each family anonymously write down their total debt (not including a mortgage). Collect the cards and add up the total debt load of the class. Compare this figure with the debt load you calculated in week 3. Celebrate any victories!

3 minutes Weekly Victory Story

Ask: Who has a special victory story to share this week?

Example: completed a Baby Step, paid off a debt, got a great bargain, had an emotional or relational breakthrough with money, etc.

4 minutes Wrap Up

Don't Forget! (from page 177 of the member workbook)

1. Financial Snapshots and the Testimonial Survey should be turned in (if on paper) or completed online.
2. Tell your class members how to start a new class in the area.

Online Features

Remind everyone to take advantage of the special online resources for *The Great Misunderstanding* at daveramsey.com/fpumember.

online resources™

Be sure to check out the special online features for this week.

- **Share It!** Find out how you can personally impact others who desperately need Financial Peace in their lives.
- **From Welfare to Independence:** Check out this inspiring two-minute mini-documentary about one woman's struggle for financial freedom.
- **My Total Money Makeover:** Take your money makeover to the next level and continue to enjoy our online money tools with our exciting online community, My Total Money Makeover!
- **Start a Class:** Learn how to start a new FPU class in your area!

Class members to check up on this week:

____

____

____

____

____

Dave Ramsey's Financial Peace University

Frequently Asked Questions

The information provided in these Frequently Asked Questions represent the most common questions we receive from class coordinators. Additional information can be found in the FAQ section of the FPU workbook. If you have a question that is not covered here, please contact your FPU Advisor.

1. **I think my class is larger than average—maybe 50 or more families. Are there any special considerations for extremely large classes?**

   An extremely large class is a great problem to have! There is an easy solution to this challenge. First, we suggest that you have the entire group meet together for the first part of each class. That way, the whole group can enjoy a sense of community as they watch the lesson DVDs together. Then, the large group should break up into smaller discussion groups of about 10-25 people. This small group dynamic is essential to a successful class and it ensures that everyone will have a chance to speak up.
   Of course, this means that you will need additional volunteer co-coordinators to lead each individual discussion group. Call your FPU Advisor if you need additional coordinator guides.

2. **As a class coordinator, do I need to buy my own membership kit?**

   You will need an FPU Leadership Kit, which includes everything you need to have a successful class. The Leadership Kit includes the complete set of lesson DVDs that you will use each week, as well as your member workbook, coordinator guide, and everything that is included in the basic membership kit. It is generally not necessary for the class coordinator to purchase an additional membership kit for personal use, as long as you have access to the workbook and other materials in your Leadership Kit.

3. **What materials will I need for my class?**

   You will need an FPU Leadership Kit, television, and DVD player. **Every family in your class will need a membership kit**. Besides that, you just need a room, some chairs, and a passion for changing lives!

4. **What is a class code? Why do I need it? Where do I get it?**

   Every FPU class has a unique class code. This code enables us to track your class' progress, successes, and history with our program. This code also acts as your class' admission into the online Member Resource Center. When you set your class dates with our office, your FPU Advisor will provide you with your class code. You'll then need to share the code with your class members so they can access the Member Resource Center.

   While the class code identifies your specific class, your information will never be sold or distributed outside our office in any way.

5. **What is the Member Resource Center (MRC)?**

   The FPU Member Resource Center (MRC) is a fantastic online resource that provides you with additional tools, content, and special features as you work through *Financial Peace University*. Each week of your 13-week class, the MRC offers you fresh insights on the FPU lessons, helpful reminders and budget tips, encouraging testimonies, and MRC-only special offers. Plus, you'll have access to these powerful features:

   - Online budget software to simplify your monthly cash flow plan, debt snowball, expense tracking, and more!
   - Exclusive, interactive teaching videos that bring clarity to the FPU concepts by showing you exactly how to apply them to your life!
   - Community message forums, where you can interact with other FPU members around the world!
   - Online Financial Snapshot form to help track your progress through the 13-week class!
   - Downloadable versions of all the budget forms used throughout FPU!
   - Extensive interactive glossary that demystifies hundreds of financial terms and concepts!
   - Up-to-date statistics and geographic information!
   - Regular contests and giveaways!

6. **How long will I have access to the Member Resource Center?**

   All FPU members, including class coordinators, have complete access to all of the wonderful resources of the MRC for 15 weeks, which easily takes you throughout your first FPU class experience. After 15 weeks, you will still have access to the teaching content and lesson-related material.

7. **How do I join the Member Resource Center? How do my class members join?**

   It's easy! Be sure to get your specific class code from your FPU Advisor and go to daveramsey.com/fpumember. Click the "Get Started Now" button on the homepage and follow the onscreen instructions, entering your class code when prompted. During your first class session, be sure to distribute this code to your class members. They will need this in order to register for the MRC themselves.

8. **Who do we contact if we have a problem with the MRC?**

   First, please review our Frequently Asked Questions page. You can access this page by clicking the "FAQ" link at daveramsey.com/fpumember. In the FAQ, we have tried to answer most common questions regarding the Member Resource Center. If you cannot find your answer, please send us an email stating your name, MRC username, and a description of your problem. All support questions regarding the MRC should be sent by email to mrc_support@daveramsey.com.

9. **What is My Total Money Makeover (MyTMMO)? As a class coordinator, do I get a discount?**

   MyTMMO takes your MRC experience to the next level with even more exclusive online tools! MyTMMO members have ongoing access to our online budget tools and a passionate community with active message forums and live chats. MyTMMO will walk with you through the Baby Steps, tracking your progress, offering encouragement and support, and celebrating your victories. Plus, MyTMMO members can download or podcast all three hours of *The Dave Ramsey Show* in CD-quality, commercial free mp3 every day!

   As an FPU class coordinator, you will receive a complimentary one-year membership to MyTMMO. Be sure to get your free registration code from your FPU Advisor when you set your class dates.

10. One of my class members thinks he/she should declare bankruptcy. What should I do?

Bankruptcy is a horrible, gut-wrenching experience that Dave almost never recommends. In nearly every case, Dave finds that there are usually things someone can do to avoid bankruptcy. There are options most people have never examined that could actually prevent this nightmare from happening.

If someone in your class is on the brink of filing a Chapter 7 or 13, please have them consult one of our certified financial counselors through our website, daveramsey.com, or by calling 888.22.PEACE (73223) before they make that final decision.

11. Someone in my class needs more help than I can offer personally. What are our options?

First, simply love and support the hurting individual. Second, remember that you are there to help lead the class discussions, not to act as a financial counselor. If someone in your class needs additional help or has detailed questions that you are unable to answer, you should encourage them to contact a trained financial counselor. We would be happy to help connect you to a professional counselor in your area. You can learn about our counseling services at daveramsey.com.

12. Can my class members call the FPU office and get free help with their budgets?

We've packed a ton of on-demand resources into the Member Resource Center, My Total Money Makeover, and daveramsey.com. There's a good chance they'll find an answer to their questions there. Because of the sheer volume of FPU members, we simply cannot offer free one-on-one counseling over the phone. We do, however, have several counseling options available, including connecting individuals with a trained financial counselor in their area. You can learn about our counseling services at daveramsey.com.

13. Can I come to your office for one-on-one financial counseling?

Yes! You can schedule a personal, fee-based counseling session at our Brentwood, TN office by calling 888.22.PEACE or emailing us at counseling@daveramsey.com. You can also find a counselor that has been personally trained by Dave's team by visiting daveramsey.com.

14. Is it okay for a family to come to class together if they only purchased one kit?

Sharing a single kit is appropriate for engaged or married couples only. Our program is designed for families to do together, so parents with children still living at home are welcome to bring them to class, as well. Extended family members or adult children should, of course, purchase their own class materials.

15. **My *Dumping Debt* audio CD only has half of the lesson on it. Why?**

The *Dumping Debt* lesson is made up of two CDs—Part One and Part Two. Both are available in your audio CD collection that is included with your membership kit.

16. **If my class members complete the Financial Snapshot and Testimonial Survey online in the MRC, do they also have to turn in a paper copy?**

No, members who complete their Testimonial Survey and Financial Snapshot online should not turn in a paper copy of these forms.

Incidentally, we strongly encourage all class members to take advantage of the online forms. This allows faster processing and more accurate record keeping.

17. **A former FPU graduate wants to re-take FPU by coming to my class as part of his/her lifetime membership. Is that okay?**

Absolutely! As part of our lifetime membership program, an FPU member may take any live FPU class at any time. In these instances, the former graduate's old class workbook will serve as his or her admission to your class.

18. **Someone in my class has an older version of the FPU membership kit and workbook. Can they upgrade to the latest class materials?**

If someone comes to your class with an older version of the FPU membership kit, he or she has the option of upgrading to the latest version of our class materials at a discounted price. Contact your FPU Advisor for details.

Of course, this member is welcome to attend your class at no additional cost with his or her older materials, should they choose not to upgrade.

19. **Are visitors allowed to sit in on the class?**

Yes! Each member is encouraged to bring a guest to check out a single class session. Some FPU members bring a new guest to class each week! As long as each guest only attends one class, we're fine with it.

The best opportunities to invite a guest are probably Week One's *Super Saving* (the guest may decide to join the class right then and there!) and Week Four's *Dumping Debt*.

20. The DVD for tonight's lesson is damaged and won't play! What do I do?

If you discover that your Leadership Kit contains a defective DVD and do not have time to get a replacement before that class, simply skip that lesson and show the next week's lesson instead. Contact your FPU Advisor at 877.378.2667 and we will send out a replacement DVD immediately.

21. When I watch a DVD lesson, I see black bars across the top and bottom of my television screen. Why?

The FPU DVD lessons are presented in widescreen format (16:9 ratio). As such, many televisions will insert black bars across the top and bottom of the screen to preserve the correct aspect ratio. Don't worry—this is perfectly normal!

22. I need to miss a class session. Is it okay to put another class member in charge for one week?

As the class coordinator, it is vital that you attend class every week. However, in the event that you are unable to make it to class, it is best to find a replacement coordinator for that week. This could be a class member that you've grown to trust or another leader in your organization that would be willing to step in.

23. Are the lesson DVDs accessible for the hearing impaired?

Yes! Each lesson DVD has three options: standard closed captioning (CC) on CC-enabled televisions, subtitles, and American Sign Language (ASL).

- CC is available for compatible televisions connected via S-video or composite connections. DVD players connected via HDMI or component cables are not supported.
- Subtitles can be activated from the "Setup" menu or turned on/off with the "Subtitle" button on most DVD player remote controls.
- ASL is available in the DVD "Setup" menu. Note: ASL is available only for Dave's on-stage presentation. The brief introduction to each lesson has no ASL component.

Dave Ramsey's Financial Peace UNIVERSITY

Additional Materials

Coordinator Recommended Reading List

One of the defining characteristics of wealthy people is that they read at least one non-fiction book each month. If you are interested in learning more about getting out of debt, building wealth, and becoming the person you were meant to be, we suggest reading the following books to supplement your Financial Peace materials. While we do not necessarily support everything in these books, they are fantastic reference resources that will broaden your understanding of your personal finances and your wealth-building potential.

1. *The One Minute Manager*
   by Kenneth Blanchard & Spencer Johnson
2. *The Richest Man In Babylon*
   by George S. Clason
3. *How To Get Out Of Debt, Stay Out Of Debt, And Live Prosperously*
   by Jerrold Mundis
4. *Back Off*
   by Budd Hibbs (Edited by Ben Dover)
5. *Think And Grow Rich*
   by Napoleon Hill
6. *Fresh Start!*
   by John Ventura
7. *The E-Myth Revisited*
   by Michael E. Gerber
8. *Life After Debt*
   by Benjamin F. Dover
9. *Using Your Money Wisely*
   by Larry Burkett
10. *Guide To Planning Your Financial Future*
    The Wall Street Journal, Lightbulb Press
11. *Guide To Understanding Money & Investing*
    The Wall Street Journal, Lightbulb Press
12. *Guide To Understanding Your Taxes*
    The Wall Street Journal, Lightbulb Press
13. *The Word On Finances*
    by Larry Burkett
14. *Who Moved My Cheese?*
    by Spencer Johnson
15. *Rich Dad, Poor Dad*
    by Robert T. Kiyosaki

Class Attendance Roster

888.22.PEACE
615.620.6398 (Fax)
daveramsey.com

Coordinator: ____________________ Location: ____________________

Advisor: ____________________ Start Date: ____________________

Names & Phone Numbers (Please Print)	1	2	3	4	5	6	7	8	9	10	11	12	13
John Smith (615) 555-1234	✓	✓		✓	✓	✓	✓	✓		✓	✓	✓	✓

**If a member misses 2 consecutive classes, please call them to see if everything is all right.
Please make copies as needed.

Class Attendance Roster

888.22.PEACE
615.620.6398 (Fax)
daveramsey.com

Coordinator: ______________________ Location: ______________

Advisor: __________________________ Start Date: ____________

Names & Phone Numbers (Please Print)	1	2	3	4	5	6	7	8	9	10	11	12	13
John Smith (615) 555-1234	✓	✓		✓	✓	✓	✓	✓		✓	✓	✓	✓

**If a member misses 2 consecutive classes, please call them to see if everything is all right.
Please make copies as needed.

COORDINATOR REPORT

Please make copies of both sides of this form upon graduation of each 13 week class and fax to (615) 620-6398 or mail the information to our office. This helps us keep our statistics up-to-date. For either method, please put to Attn: FPU Assistant.

Thank you!

COORDINATOR FIRST NAME

COORDINATOR LAST NAME

COORDINATOR EMAIL ADDRESS

PRIMARY PHONE NUMBER

( ) -

ALTERNATE PHONE NUMBER

( ) -

NAME OF CLASS LOCATION

CHURCH ADDRESS

CITY

STATE

ZIP CODE

-

CLASS CODE

YOUR FPU ADVISOR

HOW DID YOU FIRST HEAR ABOUT BECOMING AN FPU COORDINATOR? (PLEASE PRINT PLAINLY)

WHAT KIND OF PROMOTIONS DID YOU DO TO GET YOUR CLASS STARTED? (PLEASE PRINT PLAINLY)

IF YOU HELD AN ORIENTATION, HOW MANY DID YOU DO BEFORE THIS CLASS STARTED? ○ 1 ○ 2 ○ MORE

CLASS START DATE (MM/DD/YY)

/ /

GRADUATION DATE (MM/DD/YY)

/ /

NUMBER OF PEOPLE SIGNED UP FOR CLASS COUPLES SINGLES

NUMBER OF PEOPLE WHO GRADUATED COUPLES SINGLES

WHAT TYPE OF CLASS DID YOU HAVE? ○ BUSINESS ○ CHURCH ○ LOWER INCOME ○ MILITARY ○ SPANISH

ETHNIC MAKEUP OF CLASS:
○ WELL BALANCED
○ MOSTLY HISPANIC
○ MOSTLY CAUCASIAN
○ MOSTLY ASIAN
○ MOSTLY AFRICAN-AMERICAN
○ OTHER

IF OTHER, WHAT ETHNICITY?

BEST GUESS OF AVERAGE HOUSEHOLD INCOMES:

○ < $15,000 ○ $15 - 30,000 ○ $30 - 50,000 ○ $50-80,000 ○ $80 - 100,000 ○ $100,000+

TOTAL CLASS DEBT PAID $.

TOTAL AMOUNT SAVED BY CLASS $.

TOTAL AMOUNT OF DEBT AVOIDED BY CLASS $.

IS ANYONE IN YOUR CLASS GOING TO BECOME AN FPU COORDINATOR? ○ YES ○ NO

NAME OF POTENTIAL COORDINATOR (PLEASE PRINT)

SENT IN APPLICATION YET? ○ YES ○ NO

SUGGESTIONS, COMMENTS, QUESTIONS, VICTORY STORIES... (PLEASE PRINT PLAINLY)

DID YOU SEND IN YOUR TESTIMONY SURVEYS? ○ YES ○ NO

DID YOU SEND IN YOUR CLASS'S FINANCIAL SNAPSHOTS? ○ YES ○ NO

DOES ANYONE IN YOUR CLASS WANT A ONE-ON-ONE FINANCIAL COUNSELING SESSION? IF SO, PLEASE HAVE THEM CALL US AT 888.22.PEACE SO WE CAN HELP THEM.

IS ANYONE IN YOUR ORGANIZATION INTERESTED IN BECOMING ONE OF OUR TRAINED FINANCIAL COUNSELORS? IF SO, WHO?

FIRST NAME

LAST NAME

PRIMARY PHONE NUMBER

( ) -

HAVE YOU OR ANYONE IN YOUR CLASS CALLED INTO DAVE'S RADIO SHOW TO SHARE VICTORY STORIES ON AIR? ○ YES ○ NO

CALL 1-888-TALK-BAK (825-5225) TODAY WITH YOUR STORY!

DATE OF NEXT ORIENTATION

/ /

NEXT CLASS START DATE

/ /

PLEASE BE SURE TO FAX BOTH SIDES OF THIS INTO OUR OFFICE: 1-615-620-6398

25452